B. CUTHBERTSON
17 Fodbank View,
Dunfermline.

Favourite Children's Games

from around the world

November 1985

THE COUNTESS OF MAR AND KELLIE

Favourite
Children's Games

from around the world

RICHARD DREW PUBLISHING

GLASGOW

First published 1984 by
Richard Drew Publishing Ltd
6 Clairmont Gardens
Glasgow G3 7LW

All royalties are being given to the
Royal Scottish Society for the
Prevention of Cruelty to Children

British Library Cataloguing in Publication Data

Mar and Kellie, *Countess of*
Favourite children's games
from around the world
1. Games—Juvenile literature
I. Title
790.1'922   GV1203

ISBN (Cased) 0 86267 083 7
(Paperback) 0 86267 074 8

Editor: Antony Kamm
Design by J.W. Murray

Printed and bound in Great Britain by
Cox and Wyman Ltd., Reading

Typeset in Souvenir Light by John Swain Glasgow Limited

For
Clive and Helen

---

who gave their great-aunt
a big red notebook
for Christmas

Contents

Established 1884

Foreword

THIS BOOK began when I wrote to tell two of my very young relations that I would make a big jotter they had just given me into a games book.

I am lucky enough to have friends dotted around the world, so I asked them for games played in their countries. Then I asked friends in the UK and some Groups with whom I am much involved for their favourites. These, plus our family favourites – some old as the hills, others our own invention – are here for you to adopt and adapt.

'Quick, think of a game we can play at once,' is an SOS which I hope this book will answer, depending on whether you are faced with two hundred small children clamouring to come inside for a Community Centre party or wondering how to keep the family interested on a long, long journey so that the driver can concentrate undistracted by apparent chaos going on in the back seats!

The best games do not need elaborate equipment or complicated preparation and have no language barriers. One evening when it took the electrician in Bulgaria two and a half hours to mend the fused bedroom lights, my twins and I spent the time playing 'Old Maid' in the foyer with ten complete strangers, without a word of English between them, who had never seen the game before. I also remember keeping some small Norwegian boys amused on a boat trip playing 'Squares' when conversation was impossible.

The golden rule is to avoid making anyone feel small in their own eyes and those of their contemporaries or to endure the misery of being the last to be picked for a team! It only needs a little imagination to ensure that games are fun for all, players and onlookers alike.

I am startled by the number of people who have no recollection of ever having played a game other than 'cawing a gird', skipping or bouncing a ball off the wall. Several more friends have tried very hard to help but have been unable to find any local games.

Without the help and encouragement of so many friends and groups, this book would never have come into being. Most particularly my thanks go to:

HRH The Princess Margaret, President of the RSSPCC for her encouragement;

Commander Cyril Whittington and Mr Arthur Wood, for advice when the book was still only an idea;

Mrs James Atkinson, who helped with the arrangement of the games;

Mr Antony Kamm for his editorial skilled expertise;

and Mrs William Walker, who endlessly typed, sorted and proof-read the games.

All royalties go to the Royal Scottish Society for the Prevention of Cruelty to Children to help them continue their work among vulnerable children.

Panny Mar and Kellie

The Contributors

Mrs Norman Kettles 102
Mrs Alistair Lean 78, 89
Mr Richard Lunt 39, 84, 112
Mrs C.P. Mackie 118
Mr Gavin Mackie 82
Miss Tara Mackie 26
Lady Phyllis MacRae 60
The Rev. Douglas Mansill 54(2), 152
Countess of Mar and Kellie 15, 19, 20, 31, 86, 91, 93,
    106, 124, 135, 141
HRH The Princess Margaret 71, 72
Miss Rosie Marshall 151
Miss Anne Matthews 70, 99, 103
Mrs M.P. Michaelides 114
Countess of Northesk 140
Miss Anne O'Connell 109
Fru Christian Olsen 44, 47
Frøken Ingse Olsen 42
Sister Philippa OHP 142
Mrs John Robertson 76
Mrs Marion Russell 34
The Rev. Gordon Simpson 156
Mrs Mona Smith 65
The Rev. Dr Roderick Smith 67
St Mungo's (Alloa) Youth Workshop 113
Lady Torphichen 25, 57, 115(2)
Mrs Ramsey Tullis 120, 121(2)
Signora Cleme Vefling 66
Mr William Walker 68
Mrs William Walker 122
Commander C.W. Whittington 81, 94, 104
Mr Arthur Wood 107, 123
Youth-at-Risk Advisory Group 92
Mrs Stanley Zak 129, 134, 154
Mr S. Zaklukiewicz 58

Ice-Breakers

Tommy

One player goes out of the room and the others lay out five or six sweets on the floor – choosing one sweet to be 'Tommy'.

The player then comes back into the room and takes the sweets until Tommy is picked up – he is then 'out' and another player goes out of the room; and so on until everyone has had a turn.

The winner is the one who has collected the most sweets.

Sheep dogs

All players are in the middle of the room and one person catches another by the hand. They then either run round in pairs, or they make one long chain. Anyone who is caught joins the train, and so on until everyone gets involved.

I'm a train

One person starts off by running round the room saying, 'I'm a train, toot-toot,' and then stops in front of someone and says, 'Toot-toot, my name is . . . . What's yours?' That player says what their name is and goes in front. They then stop at the next player and say, 'Toot-toot, my name is . . . . What's yours?' The one in front always has to try and give the names of all those following. The new player always goes out in front, and if they get stuck they can be helped out by the others.

It does mean you quickly get to know the names of those present.

Lucky handshake

EQUIPMENT: *a minute prize.*

Everyone is told that someone has the 'lucky handshake', and they must rush around and shake the hand of as many others as possible in the hope that they will get the lucky handshake.

Arrange with one of the party to choose a number in advance and then to announce the lucky one as being that number to shake them by the hand.

Laughing handkerchief

'This hilariously silly game only needs a handkerchief and any number of people.'

One person throws a handkerchief into the air — when it starts to fall everybody must laugh, but when it lands there must be silence. Anyone still laughing is out.

Match game

EQUIPMENT: box of matches.

On arrival each person is given five matches and told to talk to people in the room and try to make them say 'yes' or 'no'. Each time anyone says 'yes' or 'no' he gives a match to the person talking to him. At the end of ten minutes or less, the person with the most matches is the winner.

'Thoroughly irritating, but it really makes people talk.'

Bleep, bleep

Players are paired off and decide upon a signal. They then scatter around and with eyes closed try to find their partner by hearing their signal.

Choosing partners
from Chile

Two circles, one inside the other, revolve in opposite directions. When the music stops, or a whistle blows, the circles stand still and your partner is immediately opposite you.

While the circles are moving they can sing, dance or do anything else to give a whole variety of movement, but it ensures partners are chosen without anyone being left to the last!

Get knotted

Equipment: lots of small lengths of wool, any colour, dotted around the house, if possible.

Pair the players off, then tell them to hold hands and go and find two bits of wool. While still holding one of each other's hands, they must then try with their other hands to knot the wool — any knot will do, granny or reef or what they like: but they must only use the one free hand that each has. The game is won by the couple who, in the time allotted, makes the longest continuously joined-up rope of wool.

Rubber-band game

EQUIPMENT: rubber bands galore.

Divide the party into groups. Set a time limit within which the groups pick up as many scattered rubber bands as they can find. Whichever group collects the most bundles of ten wins. (You can make the game more sophisticated by substituting bits of coloured wool, some colours scoring more points.)

Word of warning – do not scatter anything that will clog up the carpet sweeper, as it is amazing how many rubber bands escape the players' notice! By getting the groups to make up the bundles of ten, the judges can quickly spot the winner.

'For many years we had an annual party for Primary 7 of a local school, and the Rubber-band game became a firm favourite.'

Outdoor (or Big Hall) Games

Twos and threes

Any number can play this game. They stand in pairs one behind the other, forming a circle, except for the 'captor' and the 'fugitive'. The fugitive, in order to avoid being caught, runs in and out of the circle between, behind and in front of the couples, but can at any moment stand in front of a pair, whereupon the one at the back immediately takes over the role of the fugitive and has to start running. The whole point is that never must any pair become a threesome.

If the fugitive is caught, he then becomes the captor, and so the game can go on for as long or as short a time as anyone decides.

Cat and mouse

Cat and mouse is a game that needs plenty of space, either a big hall or out-of-doors — the only equipment is a whistle for the organiser.

The players stand in lines of four or five, according to the numbers you have, all facing the same direction and linking hands with arms outstretched.

The cat chases the mouse back and forth along the lines. When the whistle is blown the players forming the lines immediately drop hands, turn to their right and hook-up with the people now standing next to them in order to form lines at right angles — the chase still goes on with the cat and mouse diving up and down the newly formed lines.

It is essential that whenever the whistle is blown the players automatically reform the lines in the different direction.

Skatule, skatule, hejbejte se

'Boxes, boxes, get moving'
from Czechoslovakia

This game is very simple and great fun, with a lot of rushing around.

The players take position by trees, or posts, with one player spare. There must be one less tree, or post, than players. When the 'spare' player says, 'Skatule, skatule, hejbejte se', every player runs to another tree, or post, and the one who does not manage to find a free one is the 'spare' next time.

Lions and tigers

The players are split up and half sent to each end of the hall. One half are lions, the other tigers.

The leader shouts (for example), 'Lions, two paces forward.' 'Tigers, three paces forward,' etc., until they are close to each other.

Then, 'Lions chase tigers,' or vice versa. The side that is chasing tries to catch as many of the others as it can before they reach their end of the hall again. Those that are caught join the other side. The game goes on until all of one side are caught.

Red Rover

from U.S.A.

Two teams form up in lines quite a distance apart, linking hands or arms. They take alternate turns. The team captain shouts, 'Red Rover, Red Rover let (name a person) come over' – the person whose name is shouted runs towards the opposing line and tries to break through at any point they choose. If they manage to break through the line they go back to their original place, but should the team manage to catch them without breaking hands they then join the opposing team's line.

Each team takes a turn until one line has everyone in it.

Four square

A game for five players. Four of them stand one at each corner of a square of about 10 metres. The player who is 'it' stands in the middle. The others swap corners with each other, running whichever way they like, while 'it' has to get to a corner while it is unoccupied. The one left out becomes the next 'it'.

The game can also be played with seven or nine players if the extra ones take up positions in the middle of the sides of the square.

Editor's note: contributed from Tasmania. In France, this game is called 'Quatre coins'.

Na vodnika
The bogeyman
from Czechoslovakia

The idea used to be that the bogeyman would lure children into the water, and put the souls of the drowned children into cups with lids on. But once let free out of the water they would come back into their human shape.

Two sides are lined up with a space between the two teams. A bogeyman controls the 'space', and the two teams try and swap sides. While they are crossing the bogeyman's land he can catch them. Once caught the player has to sit down as a soul-in-a-cup, and the game continues until either the bogeyman has caught all the players, or, if the players are very agile, they can rescue all the souls-in-the-cups without themselves being caught.

The sea and her children

from Australia

The children stand in 'home bases' and each group is named after a sea creature. The leader, 'the sea', walks around in the middle calling, 'the sea calls the sharks', etc., until all groups are following her. If she says, 'the sea is calm', all walk on tiptoe. If she says, 'the sea is choppy', all bob up and down. If she says, 'the sea is rough', all run with arms vigorously swinging. When she says, 'the tide turns', all run to their 'homes'. She chases and catches as many as possible. Those caught join 'the sea' and try to catch the others in the next round. This continues until all have been caught.

On the quarter-deck

The walls of the room are named as parts of the ship, i.e. fore, aft, port, starboard.

The leader shouts instructions which must be obeyed, e.g. 'fore', and all the players run to wall which is fore. The last one loses a life.

Other calls: Pull for the shore (players sit and row).

Planes overhead (lie on back and pretend to use a gun).

Hit the deck (lie face down).

Up to the rigging (feet must be off the ground).

Islands

EQUIPMENT: hoops, mats, or ropes tied and laid on the floor to form circles – anything which will make 'islands' will do.

The game can be played out-of-doors, or inside – any number can play, depending on available space. An adult or a chosen child can be caller.

The players run anywhere on the floor, but must not tread on an island. The caller calls out a number – that number of players may stand on each island; any spare players are eliminated.

The game continues in this way. After each call, the number of islands is reduced – quickly or gradually, depending on the length of time you want the game to last. In the end, there must be only one island left, and the last number called must be 'one'. The player who makes it to the island first is the winner.

This game can be varied by 'forfeit' elimination – e.g. 'Everyone wearing blue socks must leave the island.'

'As a teacher, I have a teacher's fondness for relatively orderly, relatively peaceful games. This game combines a degree of order with some scope for exuberance — the compromise for which I usually have to settle!'

Have you got?

A group game for any number of players.

The players sit in their groups, and choose one to be their 'runner'. All groups must be equal distance from the leader who calls out, 'Have you got a . . . .?' (asking for something like a left shoe-lace, or a coin, etc.) The runner who gets the article quickest to the leader wins a point.

This game can last as long as needed.

Trains

Children split up into teams of say four and form 'trains' (holding each other one behind the other).

Each is allocated a railway station name: e.g. Euston, Glasgow Central, Waverley, etc., and take up positions round the room. One player is blindfolded in the middle of the room.

The leader shouts 'Euston to Waverley' and the Euston and Waverley trains must make noises like a train and change places. The player in the centre must try and catch hold of a train.

Grandmother's steps

Suitable for young children — any number of players.

One player is chosen as Grandmother and stands at the opposite end of the room with their back towards the others. Players have to try and creep up and touch Grandmother without being seen to move whenever Grandmother turns round. Anyone spotted on the move is out, and the one who reaches Grandmother undetected is the winner, and then becomes Grandmother.

Schiaffo de soldato

This Italian game got its name because boys doing their military service would play it while hanging around.

One player stands with one arm over his chest with the palm shielding his view behind, and the other across his tummy with the palm up. Rather like 'Grandmother's steps', the others have to creep up from behind and slap the lower hand. The first player then has to guess who has hit his hand, without turning round. If he guesses right, the 'hitting' player takes his place.

Blind pirate

One player sits blindfolded in centre of room with 'treasure' in front of him. The leader points to one of the players on the outside ring who must come and steal the treasure.

Player in centre listens for the player coming and is allowed to point at him. If he points directly at the player another player is chosen until all the treasure is stolen.

TREASURE

Bosse

Humps
from France

Originally played in the fields where the natural humps and hollows of the land provide good hiding places. One player is 'it' and stands at the base, a position from which 'it' can see a semi-circle of natural hiding places – small mounds, trees, clumps of bushes or flowers, a wheelbarrow, car and so on – whatever is available.

With eyes closed 'it' counts to 10. All the participants run to the first cover – or if they have time – on to the second place of cover. They must be hidden by the time 'it' has counted to 10 and opens eyes. Anyone still visible must come back to base and start again. The first person to complete the course becomes 'it' and takes over the counting.

Hide and seek

from the Isle of Iona

Any number of players can take part. One player is chosen to be 'Het' and is left at the Den to count to 100 by the five times table. Meanwhile, all other players hide, preferably where they can see the Den.

When the count is complete 'Here I come', is shouted by 'Het', who then goes to find the hiders. The hiders then must try to reach the Den without being seen or touched by the 'Het' player. If a player can touch the Den before the 'Het' player they shout 'In free', which can sometimes free the Den and allow any player already caught to hide again until recaptured.

Sardines

One player is chosen as the 'hideaway' — he then goes and hides himself. Then the other players start searching for the 'hideaway'.

As soon as a player finds the hideout he joins the hideaway, then if another player finds the hideout he then joins them. Then a fourth player, and so on until all players have found the hideout and are crammed together like 'sardines'. The game then begins with a new player as the 'hideaway'.

Happy families

EQUIPMENT: cards with names of families written on them. The names should be similar, e.g., McCrumb, McCann, McConnell or more complicated. There should also be a separate card for each member of the family — Mr McCrumb, Mrs, Master and Miss — enough in all for each person in the party.

The cards are thrown in the air and each person rushes to pick one up and by shouting discovers the rest of his family. They then sit down with Mr sitting on the floor, Mrs on top of him, then Master, then Miss (who is invariably a large person!) The last family to sit down in correct order is out and the four cards removed. The game continues until one family is the winner.

'A rowdy game.'

Giant game of musical bumps

This game can be played even with as many as two hundred players. Divide the players into two-year age-groupings in circles, but you must have enough judges.

When either the music stops or someone blows a whistle the slowest four to get down on the floor are out. (You can't do one at a time as it would take too long.)

When you have got down to about twenty finalists they become one group, and cheered on by their supporters, go on to the end. If there are a lot of finalists you probably will have to continue eliminating four at a time, and have a couple of champions!

'After we had played this the two hundred sat happily exhausted without even fidgeting, watching film cartoons!'

Tyven, tyven

'Thief, thief'
from Norway

The game is played to a Norwegian song, but once you know how to play it, you can sing along to almost any tune, whether or not you know the words. The more players, the more fun it is.

Everybody stands in pairs in a big circle, with an arm round their partner. One or two (or more) players go in the middle and when the music starts each grabs one of a pair and takes them to another part of the circle. Any player left alone now has to run around and pick another partner, while the singing goes on and on. The more players in the middle, the more movement there will be in the circle. You go on as long as you want.

'You can get rather exhausted playing this game, as well as a sore throat from singing. I have played it many times and always enjoyed it – the student orchestra I was with used to play it whenever we had a party. We could be as many as eighty people playing – aged from nine to sixty. It's a great way of mixing a group with big age-differences.'

Tyven, Tyven

Tyven, Tyven skal du hete, for du stjal min lille venn,   Tror jeg tra-la-la, tror jeg tra-la-la,
men jeg har det håp i vente, at jeg snart får en igjen.

tror jeg tra-la-la, ja, tror jeg tra-la-la. Jeg tror du står og sover og ikke passer på, min venn. jeg

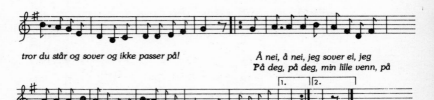

tror du står og sover og ikke passer på!   Å nei, å nei, jeg sover ei, jeg
                                                        På deg, på deg, min lille venn, på

bare står og huiler meg. Jeg sover eller våker, så tenker jeg på deg.
deg, på deg, min lille venn,   jeg sover eller våker, så tenker jeg på   deg.

Torn Rose

Sleeping Beauty
from Norway

This game is based on a very old fairy tale by the brothers Grimm and was rewritten into a song-game for children. It has been very popular ever since.

One of the players is Torn Rose, another the wicked fairy and a third the prince. All the others form a circle, holding hands, and start walking and singing:

1 Torn Rose was a pretty child, pretty child, pretty child
    Torn rose was a pretty child, pretty child.

2 In a castle she was born, she was born, she was born,
    In a castle . . . . etc.

3 Then came the wicked fairy in, fairy in, fairy in,
    Then came the wicked fairy in . . . . etc.

4 Torn Rose slept for a hundred years, a hundred years, a hundred years,
    Torn Rose . . . . etc.

5 The hedge grew very high, very high,
  very high,
  The hedge . . . . etc.
6 Then came the charming prince therein,
  prince therein, prince therein,
  Then came . . . . etc.
7 Torn Rose, you must wake up now,
  wake up now, wake up now,
  Torn Rose . . . . etc.
8 The prince is dancing with his bride,
  with his bride, with his bride,
  The prince . . . . etc.
9 All the hearts are full of joy, full of joy,
  full of joy,
  All the hearts . . . . etc.

In the first verse, Torn Rose stands in the centre while the others walk around her, holding hands and singing.

In the third verse, the wicked fairy comes into the circle.

In the fourth verse, she pushes Torn Rose who then drops to the ground. There she falls asleep while the others continue walking around and singing.

In the fifth verse they lift their arms and close the circle tightly, pretending to be a growing hedge.

In the sixth verse, the prince goes in and wakes Torn Rose up and the hedge 'withdraws'.

The prince now sings the seventh verse alone holding Torn Rose's hands – then the two dance while singing the eighth verse, and the 'hedge' stands still.

Finally everybody dances and sings to their heart's delight.

Ta den ring og la den vandre

'Take the ring and let it wander'
from Norway

EQUIPMENT: a ring.

All the players, except one, stand in a circle with their hands behind their backs. The one who is outside the circle goes round, making a movement to put the ring in each hand. The players then sing:

Ta den ring og la den vandre
fra den ene til den andre,
ringen er skjulp den sees li
nett op na er ringen has mig.
Ser du jeg har fatt den,
Ser du jeg har fatt den.
Tra la la la la la la la la . . . .

In English:

Take the ring and let it wander
from your neigbour to another.
The ring has gone, it can't be seen,
but now it is with me.
Look, I've got it!
Look, I've got it!
Tra la la la la la la la la . . . .

When they sing 'Tra la la . . . .' they put their
clenched fists in front of them. When the singing
stops, the player outside the circle asks: 'Who
has got the ring?' He then points to one of the
other players, who must say where he thinks the
ring is. If he has it himself, or if he guesses
correctly, it is his turn to be outside. If he is
wrong, the player who actually has it becomes
the new one outside.

The farmer in his den

This is played in a large room or hall with an older person at the piano.

The players form a circle with one child in the centre as the farmer. They join hands to form a ring and circle round the farmer, singing:

> The farmer's in his den,
> The farmer's in his den,
> Heigh ho my daddy-o
> The farmer's in his den.
>
> The farmer takes a wife,
> The farmer takes a wife,
> Heigh ho my daddy-o
> The farmer takes a wife.

They stop while the 'farmer' chooses a 'wife' who goes into the centre with him.

Then, 'The wife takes a child', etc., and another player goes into the centre and so on:

> The child takes a nurse, etc.
> The nurse takes a dog, etc.
> The dog takes a bone, etc.
> Heigh ho my daddy-o
> The dog takes a bone.

They all go into the centre then and clap 'the bone' on his back singing:

> The bone stands still,
> The bone stands still,
> Heigh ho my daddy-o
> The bone stands still.

The game is then repeated with a new 'farmer'.

Old Roger is dead

from Isle of Colonsay

All the players stand in a ring. One player is chosen to be Old Roger and lies on the floor. Another is chosen to be the old woman and remains in the ring. The players walk or skip round Old Roger singing:

> Old Roger is dead and gone to his grave,
> gone to his grave, gone to his grave,
> Old Roger is dead and gone to his grave,
> gone to his grave.

All the players pretend to be digging and sing:

They planted an apple tree over his head,
over his head, over his head,
They planted an apple tree over his head,
over his head.

Next, the players put their hands above their
heads and bring them down almost to the
ground pretending that apples are falling while
they sing:

The apples got ripe and all fell down,
all fell down, all fell down,
The apples got ripe and all fell down,
all fell down.

(When this was first played on Colonsay some
mischievous child tickled Old Roger at this point.
This quickly became part of the game and
always adds to the enjoyment. Old Roger seems
to enjoy it very much and squirms about
forgetting that he is supposed to be dead!)

The old woman walks around Old Roger
picking up the apples while the others sing:

There came an old woman a picking them up,
picking them up, picking them up,
There came an old woman a picking them up,
picking them up.

Old Roger then leaps up and chases the old woman around the inside of the ring pretending to kick her while the children sing:

Old Roger got up and gave her a kick,
gave her a kick, gave her a kick,
Old Roger got up and gave her a kick,
gave her a kick.

Another Old Roger, and another old woman are then chosen and the game begins again.

Odds and evens

EQUIPMENT: one ball.

Divide the players into two teams, one 'Odds' and the other 'Evens' – each team has a scorer.

One of the scorers throws the ball up in the air and whoever catches it shouts out 'Odds' or 'Evens', depending on their team. The player then tries to throw the ball to another player in the same team, which the opposing team then tries to intercept. The team which scores the greater number of catches wins.

Le ballon prisonnier

Prison ball
from France

EQUIPMENT: *a soft ball.*

For up to ten players on each side. The playing area is rectangular, with a circle in the middle and a semi-circle at each end – the younger the players the smaller the field. Toss for start, and give the ball to one team. Each player in turn throws the ball to try and hit a member of the opposite team. Anyone hit becomes a prisoner and goes to the throwing team's semi-circle. After each member of one team has had a throw, the ball goes to the surviving members of the other team.

Broken bottles

EQUIPMENT: a small ball.

The players stand, in a circle, and throw the ball to each other. Whoever drops the ball has 'broken a bottle' and must then only use the right hand for three successive catches. Failure to catch the ball again before the three catches means then using the left hand only for three successive catches. Failure again means catching on one knee, then on two knees, and finally out.

Cumán

This game has been played for a long time in Eire. Any number of players can take part. It was originally played with stones on the roads. It would be much safer to substitute soft balls or bean bags. Each player throws their ball as far as they can, the winner being the one who throws the furthest distance.

Hopping football

EQUIPMENT: *a football.*

This game is played by any number of players, who have to hop on one foot. That foot is the one used for kicking the ball!

Sock touch rugby
from New Zealand

EQUIPMENT: *two or three old socks rolled together to make a 'ball'.*

The aim of the game is to score a try by carrying the ball across a line or touching a wall at either end of the playing area.

Split into two teams of three a side or more. Play is started from the middle by running with the ball or by passing it to a member of one's own team. Opposition players must stand a yard back at the commencement of play, but may then run up and try to touch the ball-carrier.

Members of the ball-carrier's team must not drop the ball, pass it forward or run outside the playing area with ball. If they do so they must give the ball to the opposing team. Play to restart with non ball-carriers standing at least a yard back from place where infringement took place. If a member of the ball carrying team is touched he must stop and pass the ball immediately to a member of his own team.

A try equals one point.

After a try is scored play is restarted from the middle by the team that has just had a try scored against it.

Bounce ball

EQUIPMENT: an old stocking (or half a pair of tights) and a tennis ball.

Put the ball into the toe of the stocking and tie a knot to keep the ball in place. Then bounce the ball off a wall, keeping hold of the other end of the stocking. The object is to keep the ball going for as long as possible while performing different actions, e.g. sideways, up and down, between the legs, twirling around, etc. The player who bounces the ball non-stop off the wall the greatest number of times is the winner.

Stoop ball

EQUIPMENT: tennis ball or baseball.

Originally brought to the USA from Amsterdam and known as Stoep Ball. In USA the 'stoop' is the front steps leading up to apartment buildings.

Each player takes it in turn to throw the ball hard at the steps. The aim is to catch the ball without allowing it to bounce on its return. Scoring goes by the number of times the ball bounces before it is caught – the player with the least number of bounces wins. Should a player miss the catch, or the ball roll on the ground, the players waiting behind go on to play.

Palant

from Poland

This is a team game, properly played with a particular leather-covered ball. However, a tennis-ball may be used. The ball is hit by a stick or bat named 'palant'.

The game is played by two teams consisting of twelve players each, on a pitch measuring 25×60 metres. Play is over thirty minute sessions with a ten minute break at half-time.

The captains arrange the batting order of their team members and toss a coin to decide which team bats first. The aim is to hit the ball out of reach of the opposing players and run to a marker point in the middle of the playing area. If the ball is caught in one hand, then that batting player is considered dismissed without scoring a run. If the ball is not caught, when retrieved it is passed to someone near enough to hit the batting player while he is running to the marker point or back to his base line.

When all in the first batting team have played, the teams change over and runs totalled.

That is for a proper game of palant. At other

times in other situations any agreed number of players using any ball and any stick, or bat, may play. Duration of game would be decided by other circumstances such as a call to supper, or an irate farmer chasing the players away from his field!

This Polish game of Palant is of Italian origin and reached its peak in popularity at the turn of the century. It was still popular before World War Two and was one of the team games at all schools. Other games were netball and football and in spite of Palant not receiving television coverage as the two others do, it continues to be played at different times by all Polish children.

Old tin can

EQUIPMENT: tin can that can be kicked!

Suitable game for a garden with plenty of bushes near together, for hiding behind.

One player is chosen as 'He'. The tin is placed at a chosen base and while He keeps eyes closed, the others all scatter and hide. When He spots one of the hidden players and calls out their name, the one who is spotted must come out of hiding and try to get to base without being captured, in order to kick the can as far as possible. The He has to return the can to base before catching his quarry who will have tried to hide again.

If the quarry has been caught before kicking the can he is a prisoner at the base. He then goes in search of hiders, who may come out and kick the can to release the prisoner, but if caught will be prisoners. Only one prisoner can be rescued at a time, the first caught escaping first. Only one kick at the can is allowed, so He may be able to replace the can quickly enough to call out names before they can hide again, and they must then remain within sight.

Multi-ski obstacle race without snow

EQUIPMENT: skis made of thin plywood or thick cardboard with boots, or shoes, tied on to them. Two obstacles for the race course – a form to go over (as in a gym), and an obstacle to go under, like a trestle table.

Any number of teams can take part.

The teams are lined up in their skis on the starting block. On the word 'go' they start racing over the form and under the table – the winning team being the first past the finishing post, if any gets that far!

This game was played by the 1st Argyll and Sutherland Highlanders at their Christmas games in Cyprus.

Nargolyo

Seven tiles
from India

EQUIPMENT: seven fragments of tile or flat stones (or plastic dishes or bowls) that will serve to construct a roughly pyramidical pile in the centre circle; and a soft rubber ball or old tennis ball.

This is an outdoor picnic game but it could be played indoors in a hall that is spacious enough. An even number of players are divided into two teams and whichever one of them wins the toss becomes Team A, taking the strike.

Team A: Each player is allowed three tries to strike and upset the pile of seven tiles – the strike is valid even if it dislodges only the topmost tile. If an opponent takes a catch after the ball has touched the pile (even without upsetting it) the whole team is out. Otherwise all players scatter as soon as the pile has been upset to avoid being hit with the ball and got out, while one or more of them also try to get to the centre circle to rebuild

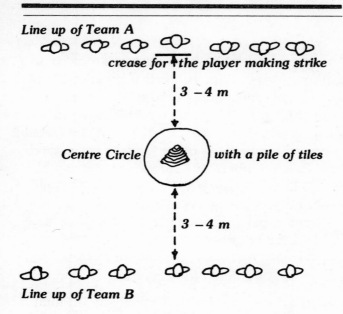

Line up of Team A

crease for the player making strike

3 – 4 m

Centre Circle *with a pile of tiles*

3 – 4 m

Line up of Team B

the pile. This may require several attempts. Once the pile has been rebuilt, the player/players achieving the feat shout 'nargolyo' and the team wins the game.

Tiles scattered within the circle.

Nargolyo!

Team B: As soon as the pile has been struck, one of the players rushes to the centre circle to scatter the tiles within the circle in a manner that will make it difficult for the opponents to reconstruct the pile. The rest of the team fan out and players pass the ball to the one who is closest to one or more of the other team to get a good aim. If all members of Team A are got out by direct hits before the pile of seven tiles is rebuilt, Team B wins the game.

'I remember when we played this game as children the boys always outnumbered the girls and we, girls, had to go through a ritual initiation of swearing solemnly to accept any rough handling we got without complaint, and to bear any injuries sustained without getting the boys into trouble. Some of us resented this and preferred not to play unless we were "exempted" from that ceremony.'

Hoist the flag

This game was played by children in the Isle of Skye, certainly up to the Second World War.

Two leaders are chosen and each picks a team from the players. On the toss of a coin the leader who wins takes their team a long way from the 'den', where the other team remains.

Having hidden the team the leader returns to those in the 'den'. Silently and by the use of hands the leader indicates where their team has gone. In using hands the leader can show how they have leapt over streams, gone under bridges and over fences, and finally settled in their 'hide'.

The second team sets off and if they have interpreted the signs will find the others. With the cry, 'Hoist the flag', both teams run for the 'den' and the other team takes its turn.

Bandiera

The flag

This is a favourite Italian game, played by two teams of at least five players each. Play is conducted by a leader, who stands in the middle of the 'playground', holding out the 'flag' (a piece of cloth) in their right hand. The two teams line up at each end of the playground.

Each player has a number (e.g. from 1 to 5 in each team). The leader calls out one of the numbers, and the two players who have this number run out to try and take the flag and bring it back behind their own line, without being touched by their opponent. If the player succeeds, that is one point to that team. If not, the other team gets the point.

A player must not go outside his own half or touch the opponent before the flag has been taken: if that happens, it is a point to the opposition.

The game continues until one team has scored ten points.

The game of the buttons

Children in the Island of Lewis played this game in the long summer evenings.

A stake is placed in the ground and the players stand about six yards from it. Each in turn pitches a button and the three nearest the stake are allowed another try.

After that the two nearest try and the best of these two is declared winner and collects all the buttons.

Cattie and doggie

EQUIPMENT: a piece of kindling wood approximately 4 inches long by $\frac{3}{4}$ inch square, and a stick some 2 feet long cut from a bush or tree.

The 'cattie' has the figures 1, 2, 3 and 4 marked one on each side, and its ends tapered to points.

A small hole is made in the ground, 3 inches across and 1 inch deep. The 'cattie' is placed with the tapered end extending over the hole – this is tapped with stick, causing the 'cattie' to jump. When it lands on the ground, the side uppermost shows a number, which entitles the player to that number of hits. The tapered end is again tapped to make the 'cattie' jump as far as possible. The other players try to catch the 'cattie' in flight: if it is caught then the catcher takes over with the doggie from the base hole. If the 'cattie' is not caught, the player carries on with any further hits due to him. The winner is the player who hits the 'cattie' the greatest distance as paced in a straight line from the base hole.

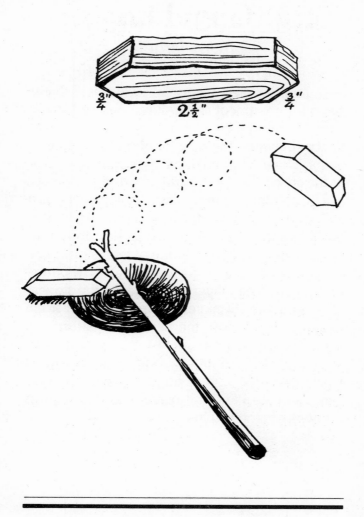

Gogohim

from Israel

This game is called 'Gogohim', which is Hebrew slang for an apricot stone. It is a national street game played by boys and girls, both Jews and Arabs, between the ages of about 6 and 10 years. The equipment is as many apricot stones as the child can collect during the apricot season.

The children form a circle. Each player has a collection of stones and has to put one in the middle of the circle. A person is then chosen to begin. They have to flick one of their stones into the middle and try to move as many of the others as possible. The player then takes all the stones that he moves. All players then put another stone in the middle before the next player's turn. When all one's stones are lost, that player is out.

The game continues till one player has collected all the stones, or, at a given time, the game can stop and the player with the highest number of stones wins.

House Games –
Non-boisterous!

Rockaway

Card game for two people, each with seven cards. Object: to get rid of them by following suit or number.

Aces are jokers and can be used to change the suit. If you can't follow suit or number, you draw till you can. If the draw pack is finished, play out the cards in your hands as best you can, following suit or number.

Scoring is over six games. If you are left with cards, they are counted face value – Aces 15 – all against you, and go on to your opponent's + score, and vice versa.

Pope Joan

Pope Joan is an ancient card game which is best played by 4 – 8 players. (Presumably it was named after the mythical woman who through her religious fervour and mastery of disguise was said to have been elected Pope in the Dark Ages.) Counters may be used instead of coins in which case each player should start with the same number of counters.

The players sit round a special board – circular in shape – standing on a stem and with the revolving bowl divided into a number of compartments. (The boards are often beautifully decorated but are rarely seen nowadays; in extremis the board can be dispensed with.)

Place in each compartment the corresponding card or cards from the suit of Diamonds; a number of packs may need to be cannibalised for this purpose. The compartments are: Pope Joan (the nine of Diamonds); The Ace, the King, the Queen and the Knave of Diamonds; Matrimony – The King and Queen of Diamonds; Intrigue – The Queen and Knave of Diamonds (also known as Malice). Some boards have a further compartment called Game – presumably to collect a bonus for the winner.

The game begins with all players 'buttering the board'. This involves placing two counters in Pope Joan and one in each of the other compartments. In all subsequent hands, each player puts one counter into Pope Joan, except for the player on the left of the dealer, who has to butter the board.

The dealer – the deal passes one place to the left with each hand – deals out a pack of cards from which the eight of Diamonds has been removed. He retains the last 3 or 5 cards (5 makes a better game) as 'stops', of which only the top one is turned up – the remainder may only be looked at by the dealer. (Some players will thus have more cards than others.) If the top stop is a Diamond, then there are 'prizes'; this means that any player who in the normal course of play can put down the card or cards corresponding to one of the compartments of the board, may claim the contents. The only exception to the 'prizes' rule is Pope Joan, the counters in whose compartment can be claimed if she is played whether the top stop is a Diamond or not.

The winner of each hand is the player who is

able to play all their cards. The lead is made by the player on the left of the dealer – for example the Ace of Diamonds. (Each player places the cards they have played in a pile in front of them.) The player with the two of Diamonds will play it, to be followed by the player with the three of Diamonds and so on until either the dealer says 'stop' because the following card is a stop, the suit is exhausted or, in the case of Diamonds, when the seven has been reached, because the eight has been removed. (The removal of the eight of Diamonds is to prevent leading up to Pope Joan.) Suit must always be followed. The next lead is made by the player of the last card and the hand continues until a player has managed to play all their cards. Each of the other players pays to the winner of the hand one counter for each card they have left, unless they are left with Pope Joan, in which case the payment is doubled.

The game continues until all players bar one are bankrupt, but more usually until by common consent play has continued long enough. (Play is often prolonged by loans between players or from the 'bank' of counters.) In the latter event, a final hand is played with 'prizes' automatically (no matter what suit the top stop) and is preceded by a universal buttering of the board. Any prizes left at the end are dealt for. The winner of the game is of course the richest.

Hints for play:

1 Lead out Pope Joan as soon as you can unless you are certain to obtain the lead again.
2 Lead out your Aces since they cannot be led up to.
3 Lead from as low down as possible in your longest suit.
4 Remember what has been played and what stops have been announced; this will guide your leads.
5 If you are dealer, use your knowledge of the stops.

Old Maid
or Mossy Face

EQUIPMENT: one or two packs of cards depending on the number of players. Any number can play.

Remove one Queen from the pack then deal out all the other cards. Players look through their cards and throw into the middle any pairs of cards. Then, in turn, they offer their cards to the next player to choose one, and if it makes a pair they throw it into the middle. Players keep their cards facing themselves. The 'Old Maid' is the player left with the odd Queen.

The alternative, Mossy Face, is the same game, but an unknown card is removed – but it is much less exciting than Old Maid where the 'dangerous' card is known to be doing the rounds!

The chocolate game

You will need a large bar of chocolate, a knife, fork, an unbreakable plate, a small table and a dice.

Sit everyone in a large circle. Put the chocolate on the plate on the table with the knife and fork, and set all this in the middle of the circle.

The dice is passed round and the first one to get a six runs as fast as he can to cut a square of chocolate and goes on eating squares of chocolate until someone else throws a six.

The game then continues until all the chocolate is finished.

Up Jenkins

Two teams sit on either side of a table. One team takes a coin and a chosen player hides it in their hand, e.g., between fingers.

The opposing team have to guess who has the coin – they say, 'creepy crawly', which means the team with the coin have to make their fingers creep along the table; or they say, 'slap bang', which means the hands have to be slapped flat on the table – or any other amusing instruction.

Three guesses are allowed, and a correct guess gains a point.

The idea is for all the players in the team with the halfpenny to disguise whether or not they have the coin.

The 'fist' Game – scissors, paper, rock

A game for two players and an 'umpire'.

Each player makes a fist (curls their fingers up into a ball). The players then count together '1–2–3' and on the count of 3 they do one of three things. They can hold their hand out flat – this is called 'paper'. They can leave their hand as a fist – this is called 'stone'. Or they point out two fingers – this is called 'scissors'.

Paper wraps up stone, stone blunts scissors and scissors cuts paper. So each time there is a winner, unless both players do the same thing in which case no-one wins.

This game was introduced to British Officer Prisoner of War Camps in Germany during the 1939–45 War, by the Maoris from New Zealand who were captured in Crete in 1941. It served to pass the time, particularly when the POWs were kept on parade for long periods while the Germans attempted to establish how many were missing following escapes!

The game was played at great speed, with the two protagonists steadfastly staring into each other's eyes in order to mesmerise the opponent into doing the wrong action repeatedly – which often happened.

A third person acted as 'umpire' and kept the score of 'wins' – also the time. A game would last for one or two minutes.

The winner finally slapped the loser's wrist – in a friendly way!

Clichés

Write the Alphabet down the left-hand side of the page, then choose a letter and write it in front, so you have CA, CB, CC, etc. You then have 10–15 minutes to think of things that go together with no word in between, e.g., Crystal Ball, Covent Garden, Choral Eucharist, Club Bore, etc.

You can think of as many as you like for each letter. Score as you please.

Drop the broom handle

EQUIPMENT: ordinary broom handle. Two players and one umpire. Very little space needed.

Player A holds the broom handle in front of their body horizontally, approximately waist high.

Player B faces A, and places one hand over the centre of the broom handle but clear of it.

When both players are ready, Player A will drop the broom handle and Player B will attempt to grab it before it hits the floor. The game can be played with a number of different items such as a playing card, which must be grasped between thumb and forefinger.

It is sometimes an advantage for the umpire to say, 'Ready, drop!'

Match contest

EQUIPMENT: matches, piece of paper.

A game for two people. Can be played anywhere.

Set up:

One player on each side of the board.

Aim: to move all matches from your side of the board.

Method: players alternately move the matches in an anti-clockwise direction. In one move a player lifts all the matches in one square and drops one match in each of the following squares anti-clockwise. If the last match dropped lands on a shaded square then that player receives an extra go. All matches that land in the shaded squares are no longer used.

Watch out: you may have less matches on your side than your opponent but that is not necessarily an advantage!

Editor's note: this game, sent in from Tasmania, is a version of Oware on page 142.

Side A

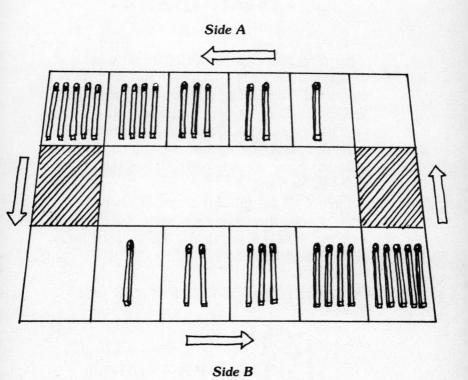

Side B

Hangman

A game for two. One player thinks of a word and writes on a piece of paper a dash for each letter of that word. The second player starts guessing the letters – A, B, C, D, etc., and if he gets a letter which appears in the word it is written in its place – this one letter may appear two or three times. If a wrong guess is made with a letter, the player starts to be hung.

First of all the ground is drawn, then the upright post, then the cross-piece, the diagonal bar, the rope coming down, then a stick man limb by limb.

For example say – HANGMAN is the word chosen.

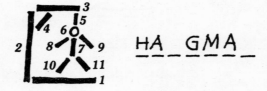

HA _ GMA _

If the word is guessed before it is completed a point is won.

Cross–words

This is a game for two players; each makes a square like this:

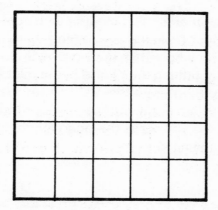

Each in turn chooses a letter which *must* be used in one of the boxes. The idea is to make up words, either across or down. You start with high hopes, but these are usually dashed by your opponent. Score 5 for five letter word, 4 for 4, etc.

Squares

EQUIPMENT: pencil and paper. For up to four players.

Someone marks out the paper with dots. In turn each player makes a line joining up two dots. Any player who puts in the fourth side claims the square by putting their initial in the middle of it, and they then draw the first line for the next square. When all the dots have been turned into squares the winner is the one with the most squares initialled.

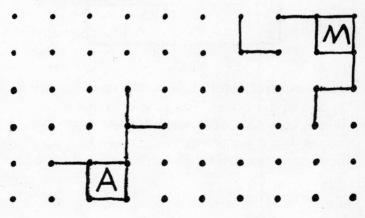

The Sunday game

'My mother was brought up to believe that only paper and pencil games could be played on a Sunday. This was passed on to her children and so to mine but we were not as strict as they were in 1880.'

Make a list on the right-hand side of the page, each person nominating something in turn up to twenty categories, e.g., Painter, Fictional Hero, Country House (my mother always insisted on Old Testament Character, O.T.C. for short!) A letter is chosen and the players have to think of and write down a name in each category beginning with that letter. 10 points is scored if nobody has your chosen word – 5 points if one other has it and no points if more than two. About ten minutes should be allowed.

Editor's note: in some families, this popular game is better known as 'Categories'.

Drawing consequences

Each player writes on the top of a large sheet of paper a title such as 'Royal Wedding', 'The Wimbledon Finals', 'Romeo and Juliet'. The paper is passed on and the next player must draw it. Before the paper is then passed on, the title must be folded back. The next player has to guess and write down what the drawing represents before that is folded back and another drawing done. And so on to the end of the page.

Telegrams

Twelve letters are chosen at random, or a twelve-letter word used. Then a subject is thought of such as 'congratulations', 'excusing oneself for missing a train', etc. Everyone writes a telegram of twelve words each starting with the letters chosen in the same sequence.

Word game

EQUIPMENT: dictionary, paper and pencil.

All players sit in a circle. One person is chosen and is handed a dictionary from which he chooses an unusual word, e.g. Pettifog or Gobemouche . . . the player spells it out for the benefit of the participants.

If you want to spin out the game, a piece of paper and pencil is given to a player who writes down what they consider is the meaning of the word, then turns it over and hands it on to the next player, and so on. This continues round all the players. However, it is quicker if every player has a pencil and paper to write out their own meaning of the word.

The player who has the dictionary then reads out the correct meaning of the word, i.e. Pettifog – practising legal shark, any quibble about small matters. Gobemouche – a fly catcher (bird), a credulous person.

Twenty questions

All players sit round in a circle.

One player thinks of a person – limit the list to famous people. The 'thinker' goes round each player who in turn asks a question which must be answered by 'Yes' or 'No', e.g., Is this person alive or dead? One question is asked by each player in turn until someone guesses the correct answer.

A player cannot hazard a guess and ask a question together.

The player who guesses correctly is the one who thinks up the next mystery person. If you hazard a guess when it is your turn and it is wrong you are out.

Secretaries

EQUIPMENT: pencils and paper; cut-out paragraphs from newspapers on different subjects.

This game is for indoors – noisy but without running around!

The players divide into pairs – one as the Secretary, the other as the 'Office Boss'. The secretaries line up at one end of the room, either sitting on chairs or the floor, and the bosses at the other end. On the word 'go' the bosses dictate a paragraph to their secretary, which the secretaries try and write down. As all the bosses are 'dictating' at the same time the paragraphs get very garbled!

At half-time they reverse roles and the winner is the couple whose paragraphs most resemble the original!

Putting on a broadcast

EQUIPMENT: *lots of newspapers and scissors.*

Divide the party into groups and ask each to prepare an 8-minute news programme for broadcasting, from the newspapers. The groups choose their Presenter, Sports Reporter, Foreign Correspondent, etc., but all should be involved. Given a set time for preparation, they must be ready to do their broadcast for exactly the length of time chosen. Points are given for presentation, news value, originality, etc.

Youth-at-Risk has found this a very good way of getting teenagers to gel quickly in groups.

People and places

EQUIPMENT: postcards or pictures stuck on sheets of paper scattered round the house, or room. Number them on the sheet.

Players are in pairs and each couple is handed a blank list which has been numbered and asked to fill in what each picture represents as quickly as possible – as they will not want to help others they have to work quietly.

Start the couples off at a different serial number so that too many are not all looking at the same sheets.

Making your mark

EQUIPMENT: two smooth blocks or tins or something similar. We used to play with empty bottles – I would not recommend these for children or young people as they can be dangerous.

Clear a space about $2\frac{1}{2}$ metres square and make a straight line mark on the floor. The first competitor will now take a tin/block in each hand, stand with toes behind the line, reach forward with hands holding and supported by the tins/blocks on the ground as far as can be reached. When at maximum reach, leave one tin/block. Place the now free hand on the other hand holding the remaining tin/block and move back until you can stand up. Mark the spot reached – the next player attempts to better it.

Rules. a) Toes must stay behind the line both going forward and returning.

b) Only the block/tin must touch the floor both going forward and coming back.

Note. The items used as tins/blocks must be as smooth as possible to reduce friction otherwise it is very difficult to return to the standing position.

Excellent for teenagers.

MARK

Hunt the thimble

EQUIPMENT: a thimble.

All the players close their eyes while the thimble is hidden. On the word 'go' everyone hunts for it, and the excitement grows as any onlookers call out – 'You are warm', 'Getting warm', 'Hot' or 'Very hot', if any of the players gets near the thimble. If they move away from the thimble the onlookers call – 'You are cold', or 'Getting colder', or 'Very cold', depending on how far away they move from the thimble.

Whoever finds the thimble then takes over to hide it again for the others.

Kim's game

With children too young to write things down, show them a tray full of different objects for a few minutes then stand them in a line and ask them in turn to name an object. They are allowed three lives and then out, so one is left at the end.

Donkey

EQUIPMENT: a large picture of a donkey, a scarf and a 'tail'.

One by one the players are blindfolded, turned in a circle and given the tail to stick as near to the right place on the donkey's bottom as possible. The winner is the one who gets nearest.

Winding and unwinding

One player starts by saying, for example: 'Mackintosh'. The next says 'Mackintosh reminds me of rain'. The next, 'Rain reminds me of puddles', and so on, and on for as long as you think you can continue, for now you have to go backwards until you reach Mackintosh again.

Memory game – I went to hospital

Any number of players sit in a circle. The first one says, 'I went to hospital to have my Appendix out'; the second player repeats this, then adds another casualty or illness beginning with the letter 'B'; the next goes on to one starting with the letter 'C', and so on.

Any player who forgets the sequence or hesitates is out.

The bell is ringing

from Israel

This game is played by Arab children under the age of about 4 or 5 years. The only equipment needed is a rag!

All players sit in a circle on the floor. A player walks round the outside with the rag in his hand while everyone sings: 'The bell is ringing, the bell is ringing, get up on to your horse and go.' The player with the rag then drops it behind another player who has to get up and chase them, having picked up the rag. If the player who dropped the rag is caught before reaching the vacant place, he has to walk round the circle again with the rag while all continue to sing, 'The bell is ringing, the bell is ringing, get up on to your horse and go.' If the player is not caught, then the one chasing goes round the circle with the rag, dropping it again behind a player. The chasing is then repeated, and so the game continues till all have had a turn.

I sent a letter to my love

EQUIPMENT: a handkerchief.

The players sit in a wide circle on the floor and one chosen player has the handkerchief and walks round outside the circle saying, or singing:

I set a letter to my love, and on the way I dropped it,
I dropped it, I dropped it, I dree, I dree, I dropped it,
I sent a letter to my love and on the way I dropped it.

Then each child is touched on the head with the words, 'It isn't you', 'It isn't you', 'It isn't you'. . . . When the player comes to one they have chosen, they say, 'But it's you', and drop the handkerchief. They then run as quickly as possible round the wide circle while the person behind whom the handkerchief has been dropped has to lift the handkerchief, jump up and run round the circle to try and catch the postman who dropped the handkerchief before the postman takes the empty space in the circle.

Editor's note: this traditional game was observed being played in Hong Kong in this form, by Chinese children. It is the same as the previous game, played in Jerusalem. It is also played in France, where it is called 'La Chandelle'.

Who has the tambourine?

from Australia

EQUIPMENT: bell, keys, etc.

A quiet game where children sit in a circle. Initially the leader selects one child by name to be 'the listener' who sits blindfold in the middle of the circle and a 'tambourine' is placed behind her. The leader then points to one child who creeps up, takes the tambourine, returns to his place in the circle and places the tambourine behind his back. All the children then put their hands behind their backs and say, 'Who's got the tambourine, Jane?' (etc.). She then says, 'Have you got the tambourine, John?' She has two or three chances to guess. Whether or not the listener is finally correct, the person who has the tambourine becomes the new listener in the centre.

Pass the parcel

EQUIPMENT: a small unbreakable prize wrapped in many pieces of paper. Any number of players can take part.

Players sit in a circle and pass a parcel to each other – when either the music stops or the leader blows a whistle the person holding the parcel is out.

To heighten excitement the last four can sit back to back passing the parcel – the winner keeps the parcel.

Lila, Lila

from Israel

This game is played by Arab children under the ages of about 4 or 5 years.

All players stand in a circle holding hands, with one player squatting in the middle and looking very lonely and miserable. All sing: 'Lila, Lila, why are you sad? You can pick a friend!' The player in the middle then walks round saying, 'Not you, not you, not you,' until they stop in front of a player and say, 'But you', and then take this player and put him in the middle in place of themselves.

The game goes on until all the children have had a turn in the middle.

Rhubarb game

Sit the players in a large circle. Number or letter
them in a clockwise direction. Remember your
number or letter.

This is a game of memory and rhythm, in
which numbers or letters are changed to the
clapping of hands and knees as follows. Hands
are clapped twice, clap-clap, followed by hands
clapping knees twice, knees-knees, to start the
game. No 1 or A takes charge and calls, 'Are you
ready?' and at the cry, 'Let the Rhubarb Game
commence' starts the rhythmic clapping,
hands-hands, knees-knees – keep it going half a
dozen times to get the rhythm and a reasonable
speed, starting slowly. When all are happy, No 1
or A will pass on the control of the rhythm. On
the first strike on the knees they call their own
number, and on the second strike another active
number in the circle – for example; hands-hands
1 – 10. 10 must be alert and keep hands-hands
to get organised, then must call their own
number and pass it on: thus it would sound –

clap – clap	1 – 10, or whatever
clap – clap	10 – 2, or whatever
clap – clap	2 – 4, or whatever.

Now life gets difficult. If you rush your own number or try to pass on the control on the clap-clap part of the rhythm you are OUT, and your number becomes dormant and thus another trap. Players must not only remember their own number but also dormant numbers, as to pass on control to a dormant number is a forfeit and the player making such a call goes out.

As the number of players decreases the tempo of the rhythm can be varied with skill and experience – all kinds of combinations of words, letters and numbers can be used with great fun.

Children are usually quick to learn – parents take a little longer.

McNamara's Band

Any number of players sitting in a ring.

One player is chosen to leave the group and go out of earshot while a leader is chosen.

All the circle mime playing the same musical instrument, and hum the tune chosen by the leader, who will frequently change the instrument without being seen by the 'outsider', who stands in the middle of the circle trying to spot who is the leader.

A well-known tune – like McNamara's Band – lends itself beautifully to the game, and the secret is for the leader to change instruments when the 'outsider' is looking at the other players.

Animal game

Each player chooses a different animal and adopts a sign that can be easily recognised as portraying the animal, e.g. the monkey scratches himself; the snake is an outstretched arm with a dangling hand to represent the hooded head; the rabbit is with hands beside the head pointing upwards to portray the ears; the crocodile is both arms out in front moving up and down to portray huge jaws; and the elephant is holding your nose to represent the length of the trunk. Players can make up any other symbols providing all the players agree they can recognise the animal being portrayed! The monkey is the lowest form of life and elephant the highest. Draw lots to see who will be the monkey, and who starts off the game.

Suppose it is the rabbit. That player makes the rabbit sign and then makes the sign of another animal, say the snake – the snake immediately makes the snake sign, and then makes the sign of another animal. If it is the crocodile, the crocodile then makes his own sign and immediately makes the sign of another animal.

The point is to try and trick the elephant into

making a mistake, but if any player makes a mistake in trying to trick any of the others, that player then becomes the monkey, and whoever was the monkey takes over their role. The great thing is to become the elephant, and the elephant then goes down to being the monkey.

Simon says

All players sit around the room while one player in the centre goes to each one in turn and says, e.g. 'Simon says it has been a lovely day', and the player to whom he is speaking repeats the sentence.

Should he only say, 'It has been a lovely day', and the player repeats this after him, then he is out. The person who is out then has to take the place of the leader.

Tell Harry

EQUIPMENT: either some tiny stick-on labels, or a lipstick – to make a washable dot!

Suitable for any number of players seated in a circle.

Everyone starts off being called 'Harry'. The first player turns to his right-hand neighbour and says, 'Hullo, Harry'. The neighbour replies 'Yes, Harry?' The first one then says, 'Tell Harry', denoting the player on the neighbour's right. Should anyone hesitate or get the sequence wrong they are immediately awarded a dot which must be very visible (e.g. on chin or forehead) – and their name then becomes 'one dot', or 'two dots' if they make a second mistake. At the third dot they are out. So the conversation could run 'Hullo, Harry', the reply being 'Yes, one dot?', and then, 'Tell two dots'. The survivors are the winners!

Chinese whispers

Any number of players sit in a circle. Someone starts off by whispering a message to their left-hand neighbour who passes it on to the player on their left, and so on right round the circle. The last player announces the message they received, which is unlikely to resemble the original!

The most famous of these 'whispered messages' started off as – 'Send reinforcements, we are going to advance!' and ended up as – 'Send three and fourpence, we are going to a dance!'

Chinese charades

An acting version of 'Chinese whispers'. Players divide into two teams and one team goes out of the room.

The first member of that team comes into the room to be told by the team still in the room the 'word'. The player then has to act it to the next member of the team who is sent into the room. The next member has to copy what the first player has acted to the second player sent in, and so on until it comes to the last player, who has to try and guess the word!

Wink murder

A game for anywhere – with players sitting in a circle. Draw lots with a broken match or by drawing a card to choose one player who is the murderer – no one else in the room must know who the murderer is.

All players look around at each other and the murderer looks at someone and winks, that person counts to five and with a horrible groan falls down dead – the other players have to guess who the murderer is before they too are all killed off.

The murderer tries to kill off everyone before being seen winking at a player.

Ducky, ducky – quack, quack

No equipment needed, but it is essential that the players know each other.

Any number of players sit on chairs in a circle with one in the middle blindfolded and armed with a cushion.

The player in the middle goes round with the cushion and sits on the cushion on the knees of any of the seated players and says, 'Ducky, ducky', to which the seated player, disguising their voice, replies, 'Quack, quack'. The blindfolded player tries to identify the player on whose knees they are perched.

If they guess correctly they change roles and the other players change seats to muddle the next 'duck'.

There is a less rowdy version of the above game – Poor Pussy. The blindfolded player in the middle goes round and kneels in front of any of the seated players and says, 'Meow, meow', to which the seated player, in a disguised voice replies, 'Poor Pussy, poor Pussy', while stroking the head of the kneeling player. The blindfolded player tries to identify the player who is stroking his head.

Blindfold fly

from Cyprus

For at least three players.

One player is blindfolded and turned round several times and has to try and catch one of the other flies – all of whom are making 'Zzzzzz' noises like flies. Having caught a fly, the blindfolded fly has to guess the name of the other fly.

No words must be spoken, and the flies try and disguise their voices by 'Zzzzzz' noises.

If the blindfold fly guesses correctly, that fly becomes the blindfolded one, and so the game goes on.

Travel Games

Bus stop game

Can be played by two people waiting at a bus stop. The players guess from which direction most cars will pass before their bus arrives!

This often results in a very close finish and can be really exciting.

Beaver

This American travel game originated as a version of 'I spy', with the players spotting the most number of men with 'beaver beards'. An updated version is spotting Jeeps, VW beetles or other distinctive cars.

Car games

It is some years since we had to keep our children amused on car journeys, but I well remember taking several lively under-fives to nursery school and frequently having to stop the car to restore order in the back seat. On one of these journeys one of the small boys announced that he was going to pretend to be dead! He did this so well and for so long, that the other children were spellbound and silent all the way home.

Such peaceful moments are rare, and on longer journeys we used to play 'observation' games to help pass the time. These are variations of 'I spy' with the players deciding in advance what they are going to look for. This will depend on the type of journey and the age of the players but it can be anything from animals or vehicles to inn signs or even people with particular characteristics such as hats or umbrellas or spectacles.

Having chosen what to spot, someone is appointed referee and scorekeeper. A scale of points can be devised as you go along, rarity value scoring the highest marks. For instance if animals are the subject, elephants and giraffes will rate the highest mark, especially on motorways, and cows and sheep the lowest as they tend to come in large numbers and the driver may have to stop the car while they are counted. This tends to defeat the object of the game and is to be discouraged!

The players should each look out of their own window if possible, but if sharing a window the first person to spot the object scores the point. The winner is the player with the highest score at journey's end, and is allowed to choose the next game.

Story telling

Retell a favourite story, particularly one with repeated words, e.g., Three Little Pigs, Gingerbread Man. Children join in as the chorus.

Travelling cricket

The game can be played in teams or as individuals, depending on numbers. Number of innings must be decided prior to start.

As cars come along the person batting counts them, scoring as follows:

All cars other than white in colour **1 run**

Cars towing trailers or caravans **2 runs**

Car-carriers or huge container-lorries with supermarket names on the side (like Woolworths, Tesco, Fine Fare, etc.) **4 runs**

Things not seen often on the roads such as Rolls Royces, Bentleys, and combine harvesters etc., (obviously it depends on the country as to what is unusual and this must be decided upon before the game starts) **6 runs**

When a white car comes along the batsman is out and the next person starts counting for runs. If a white car comes along straight away, then that is a duck and the next person comes in, and so on, until the team is all out. If played with only two, then they can have about six innings each to make the game last longer.

Suitable for any age child or adult (or at least
one that can count or stay awake long enough).
If the rules are agreed on before the start of the
journey then it can be a game with no argument
and lasting a long time, thus allowing the driver a
peaceful time. Especially good for long boring
bus journeys.

The Minister's cat

Each person in turn supplies an adjective
beginning first with the letter A (e.g. The
Minister's cat was an Awful cat), then with the
letter B and so on through the alphabet.

'On the 300-mile journey to Orkney, one of
the children was sure to ask, "Are we nearly
there?" as we approached Queensferry – about
10 miles on. Mother immediately started "The
Minister's cat". Dad teased by giving long words
which nobody had ever heard of, but we were
afraid to challenge in case they were real. With a
bit of encouragement, this kept things going for
many miles.'

Car cricket

This game is played by observing the number plates of cars in front of, or passing you. Suitable for two players.

The score is the sum of the numbers, but if the Registration letters contain the following there is no score:

C=Caught   L=LBW   R=Run Out

S=Stumped   B=Bowled

e.g. AMX 456=15   but BMX 456=no score

Fix a maximum score.

Pub sign cricket

You take it in turn to go into bat and you score runs according to the number of legs on the pub signs you pass. For example, 'The Gamekeeper' would score 2, unless he had a dog with him, in which case it would be 6. The 'King's Head' scores 0 and you are out. The 'Coach and Horses' is a sure winner!

Inn signs

A simple game for the car and two players who take a side of the road each, or alternate inns, and count legs which appear in the inn signs, e.g., Duke and Drake would equal 4, so would Cat and Fiddle – make a limit of 10 on such names as Fox and Hounds, and settle for the first to reach 50 or 100.

Guessing

A game for a journey.
Someone has to describe something, for
instance, they can say it has a tail and a big head,
or it is brown, or it moves, and the others have to
try and guess what it is that is being described.

Another game for a journey.
Each player has to make up words from the
letters of the car in front, e.g. PSR. You have to
make a word starting with P and ending with R
that has an S in the middle, like poser.

Another variation is to make up a phrase with
each word starting with P, S, or R. e.g. Pleasant
Sunday run.

Buzz

Choose a multiplier, say, three, four, or five, e.g.
suppose it is four: each person in sequence
counts, one, two, three, 'buzz', five, six, seven,
'buzz', nine, ten, eleven, 'buzz'. Any player who
makes a mistake loses a life – three lives, then the
player is out.

Geography game

Any number of players – two versions.

    1 Choose a letter of the alphabet and in turn each player must give a place name – country, town, loch, river, mountain, etc., anywhere on the map. If a player misses three turns by being unable to give a place, or repeats one, they are out.

    2 Alternatively, the first player chooses a place name and the next player has to choose a place starting with the last letter of the previous player's contribution, e.g. if the first player says Edinburgh, the next player must choose somewhere beginning with H – and so on.

Themes, Theories and Traditions

Animals

This game was seen in a kindergarten in Chile. The teacher makes the noise like an animal and imitates what the animal does – the children all follow in their own fashion. It can be any animal and some of the results can be quite surprising.

For example, if it is a lion, some lions would claw and some would roar. If it is a giraffe, some would stretch for the high leaves. The children do what they fancy, and there is great scope for their imagination.

Musical movement

In Cyprus there are numerous free movement activity games for small children, accompanied by traditional songs and catchy tunes, e.g. if the leader pretends to be a butterfly, then all the children make butterfly movements and sing appropriate songs.

Wake acting

In Eire there is a tradition of acting during a Wake – the aim being to distract from the sadness of the occasion. The theme of the acting is 'new life' again.

Pop goes the Weasel – a Border reminiscence

I was brought up on a lonely Border farm and knew more animals than human beings when I was a child. So I used to play games with them. Hide-and-seek with the horses. Follow-my-leader with the pigs (they *never* followed!) Puss-in-the-corner with the cats.

But the greatest game was bringing in the cows to be milked at night. They spent the day browsing in the meadow and did not want to leave the buttercups and daisies to go into the byre. As soon as they saw me coming to open the gate, they turned their backs and wandered away to the top of the field.

How could I get them to come? I called and *called*. 'Come on, cows! Come on! It's milking-time.'

No! They would not come. They kicked up their heels and hurried away from me. 'MOO! We're not coming. MOO-MOO!'

Then one day a tramp came to the door selling

combs and buttons and laces. Nothing I wanted to buy. Except . . . what was that lying amongst the laces?

A tiny tin whistle. It cost sixpence, so I bought it.

I blew it and blew it, and tried to learn to play. And at last I could play one tune. Only one. *Pop goes the Weasel*.

I was very proud of myself and kept playing the tune over and over again. I was playing it when I went to bring in the cows at night. What happened when they heard the music? To my surprise, they lifted their heads to listen. And instead of running away, they came towards me. 'MOO! MOO-MOO!' It seemed as if they were trying to make music, too. Indeed, I am sure I saw one of them trying to dance. So I opened the gate and out they came, as meek as could be. I kept on playing and marched them safely towards the byre, and in they went, ready to be milked.

So every evening I played the same game and the same tune. *Pop goes the Weasel*. And after that I never had any trouble getting the cows into the byre.

Chestnut champion

Allow some horse chestnuts to harden. Then bore a hole through each and thread it on to a string about 30 cm long with a knot at the end, to keep the chestnut in place.

One player holds his chestnut up by the end of the string, and the other tries to break it by swinging his chestnut. They have alternate swings, until one of the chestnuts breaks and falls off the string. The winner is also the champion of the total number of 'breaks' that the loser has scored up till then.

Magic numbers

One person must be 'in the know' and that person asks the players to write down any four digits and add them together: then take away the answer from the original number. Then they are told to cross out any one of the digits in the new answer and add the other three digits together. When the final answer is given, the 'one in the know' will be able to announce which was the digit that was crossed out.

Example:

1 Four digits, say $4464 = 18$
2 $4464 - 18 = 4446$
3 Cross out one digit, 44~~4~~6
4 $4+4+6 = 14$
5 The magician can tell that the digit crossed out was 4.

The secret lies in the number 9 as a multiplier. If the final answer given is under 9, then you subtract it from 9. If it is more than 9, subtract it from 18: if it is more than 18, subtract it from 27: and so on.

'When my parents were once staying in Madeira, George Robey was in the same hotel. He knew a lot of games, and he showed my father this one because it amused him.'

Skipping rhymes

'These are some of the rhymes I remember best
from my childhood.'

Round apple, round apple,
    As round as can be
She's dying to see
    John Murphy, John Murphy,
He's dying to see
    Annie Askins, Annie Askins go round:
Up comes her dear father
    With knife in his hand
Sez, 'Give me your daughter
    Or your life I shall have.'
Who cares not, who cares not,
    For Annie loves me
And I love her.

House to let,
    Apply within,
When you go out,
    Somebody else comes in!

The wind and the rain and the wind blew high
   The rain comes blattering from the sky
Anne Jane Murphy says she'll die
   If she doesn't get a fellow with a rolling eye.

A hundrid an' ninety nine
   Ma faither fell in the bine,
Ma mither caem oot wi' the washin' cloot
   An skelpt his bare behind!

Waan toe three
   Ma Mammy caught a flea;
She saltit it an' peppered it
   An' pit it in her tea.

Kilty Kilty cauld bum,
   Three stairs up.
The wumman in the middle flair
   Hut me wi' a cup;
Ma nose is a' bleedin'
   Ma lips a' cut,
Kilty kilty cauld bum,
   Three stairs up.

Can you read this?

Y Y U R
Y Y U B
I C U R
Y Y 4 ME

Answer: Too wise you are
Too wise you be
I see you are
Too wise for me

Forfeits

Each member of the group puts a small article or token into a chosen container, like a hat. The 'victim', a blindfolded person in the middle of the group, selects one of these items from the container, states to whom he thinks it belongs, and announces the forfeit the owner will have to do to regain the item. The forfeit is declared, which may vary from counting the stars in the sky that evening to running down to the nearest post box, or whatever.

Should the 'victim' guess ownership wrongly then the article is returned to the rightful owner and the 'victim' carries out the forfeit, and continues as victim. Should he give name of real owner, after forfeit is done, that person becomes the 'victim'.

Field day

One year we had a Field Day instead of a traditional party. We asked our young guests to wear old clothes and bring a change of dry ones. In the morning they opted for either mixed football or hockey, then back to the house for an indoor picnic. We removed the dining-room table, covered the carpet with dust-sheets, and after collecting the hot food from another room, they picnicked either in the dining-room or on the stairs, while the grown-ups ate in more comfort in another room.

Teenage sons and daughters of the host families 'made the party' by marshalling the guests to and from the games' field, supervising the changing, and dishing out the hot lunch, and then took the party to a local hall, which we were lent, to watch an epic film which seemed to intrigue the Dads as much as their young! Back to the house for tea, and parents were ready to remove their happily exhausted offspring at a human hour, instead of having to set out around midnight to collect them from a late party. Over the years several young men and women have told me the Field Day was the party they most enjoyed of their childhood. I am pretty certain this was due to coming in old clothes instead of decked up in party ones, being able to let off steam all morning; and, most of all, because of the teenage team who masterminded the day.

Ducks and drakes

Find a flat round stone 5 to 7 cm in diameter and aim it towards the sea so that it will skiff across the top of the water. The player whose stone skiffs the most times before sinking is the winner.

Editor's note: This pastime 'surfaces' on the Isle of Iona as well as in New Zealand.

Special themes for parties

Some of our most successful children's parties have been when we had a special theme.

Pirate Party

All the children came dressed as pirates, and we started off with a treasure hunt. A big map of the garden was drawn with various spots marked off with a cross. To find the treasure the children had to go to each spot and find some object – we gave them a little paper bag to put them all in, following the footsteps of Black-eyed Bill the pirate. There were different coloured bits of wool from his jersey and socks, there were his liquorice bootlaces, and his glass eye (he obviously had spares), which was a marble, his sugar cigarettes and his liquorice pipe and various coloured rags from bits of his clothing. When they came back to the front door we were waiting to see that they had found everything, and then they climbed a ladder to the battlements where Black-eyed Bill himself (my

husband suitably disguised) was waiting beside
an iron treasure-chest full of gold doubloons
(chocolate coins).

After this it was time for tea, and the birthday
cake was also a large chocolate cake
treasure-chest full of gold pieces of eight and
jewels (fruit gums).

Nursery Rhyme Party

All the children came dressed as nursery
characters. We had a parade first of all, judged
by grandmothers — two enchanting children who
came as The Maiden all Forlorn and the Man all
Tattered and Torn from the *House that Jack
Built,* were first; and Mary, Mary, Quite Contrary
came second, with Wee Willie Winkie in striped
nightshirt and red cap, third.

After this we had a slightly complicated
treasure hunt in the garden, in which they all had
to do various nursery rhyme activities: hunting
for wool lamb's tails (*Mary Lost her Little Lamb*):
putting a ball at clock golf (*Hickory Dickory
Dock*): sewing a few stitches (Curlylocks 'sewing
a fine seam'): Simple Simon went a-fishing —
which was trying to hook sweet fishes from a

bucket: there were orange and lemon slices to find (*Oranges and Lemons*), jelly babies (*Hush-a-Bye-Baby*) and sugar mice (*Pussy Cat, Pussy Cat, where have you been?*). The finale was finding the Gingerbread House, which was the children's Wendy House with gingerbread hearts stuck all over it – each iced with the name of one of the guests, and sweets, sugar carrots and apples and lollipops.

The birthday cake, of course, was a Gingerbread House, iced with chocolate buttons on the roof and sugar roses climbing up the walls.

Treasure-hunting is always most popular with children, particularly if it means little presents to take home. Variations are finding the most bits of coloured wool, or Smarties or peanuts (though these tend to get eaten before the final count-up comes). Cutting old Christmas cards in half and finding the matching piece is a very useful party-starter.

Manx national games

A number of social games were played traditionally in the Isle of Man such as 'Goggins' and 'Eirinagh veih Nherin', both of which were divination games, one for girls and the other for men, regarding marriage prospects. The second of these is interesting as a relic of wife barter, for the man chooses his girl and then has to say what he will offer for her – a horse or a cow, maybe – while the rest of the players cry 'Bogh!' (Poor) until eventually the bargain is struck. Then they dance around the pair singing 'Gow dty Ven as poosee ee' (Take your woman and marry her).

Much more like a national game, however, is the traditional one of Cammag, which was formerly played regularly throughout the Island by teams of men and boys with sticks, preferably made of gorse wood, something like a hockey stick but with a rather broader blade. There were eleven players in the team, and Cammag was played not on a special pitch but between representatives of two adjoining parishes on a road or field at the parish boundary. It was quite a rough game, sometimes, in fact often, ending with some broken heads. At the end the victorious team would perform a dance with their sticks (or the survivors would!) and then were entertained to supper at a local pub by the losers. The Manx dance 'Gorse Sticks', although actually a composed one, is probably based on this game, but is a solo.

Cammag is still quite well-known today as a tradition, but is never actually played now, though it certainly was well into the present century. It is really the Manx form of the very ancient Gaelic game now known and played as an organised sport in Eire as Camogie, with its own book of rules, etc.

Collecting car numbers

Any number of players can take part. The car numbers are collected in sequence. This game can last a year, a week, or over a holiday if agreed by all the players, who must be trusted not to cheat.

The game of Oware

Oware is a general name for the board on which various games are played by dealing beans into a series of 'cups', technically known as mancala games. The earliest known mancala board consists of a set of deeply-cut holes in the stone of the Kurna Temple at Thebes. This temple was built around 1400 BC. Other boards have been found, cut in the stone of the temples of ancient Egypt: for example, at Luxor and Karnak. The boards consist of two rows of six, seven or eight saucer-shaped holes about 9 cm wide and 3 cm deep.

Mancala boards have been found in Arabia, dating back before the time of Muhammad; and it is believed that the followers of Islam carried the game to the countries influenced by their culture.

Oware boards are hand-carved from a solid block of wood and consist of two rows of six scooped-out cups, but in a village holes may be dug in the ground and small stones used in place of the traditional oware beans.

Versions of Oware are played in many parts of the world. In the American continent, the slaves originating from Africa played their native games and taught them to their children. In some cases it is still possible to trace the origins of some West Indian negroes by the form of mancala that they play.

In the New World, Oware is often called Awari. It has a religious significance and is often played at funeral celebrations to pacify the spirit of the dead awaiting burial. It is believed that making Awari boards involved spiritual danger and only old men who have lost a wife are allowed to make them.

The rules which follow are based on the method of play in Ghana and the games are referred to by their names in the Ghanaian language of Twi.

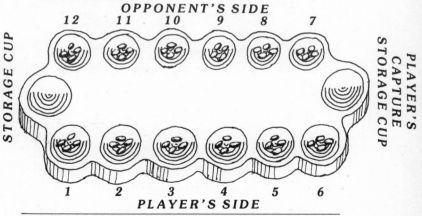

General Rules of Oware

Rule 1

The game is played by two people who will be referred to as the the 'player' and the 'opponent'. Any of the rules mentioning the player apply equally to the opponent when it is his turn, and vice versa.

Rule 2

At the start of the game, 4 beans are placed in each of the six cups on the player's side of the board and 4 beans are placed in each of the opponent's six cups, i.e. 48 beans are in use at the beginning of the game. The two cups positioned centrally at the ends of the board are left empty. These cups are to be used for storing subsequently captured beans, and are called 'capture storage cups'. Each player uses the capture storage cup on his right. (In some countries, the number of cups and the number of beans per cup is varied.)

Rule 3

The player and the opponent play alternately, having previously agreed by 'tossing' who shall make the first move in the first game. It is usual to play a series of games in which the player and the opponent alternate in having the first move.

Rule 4

The player starts his move by picking up all the beans from any one of the six cups on his side of the board. He deals them one in each cup as far as they will go, round the board in an anti-clockwise direction, starting with the adjacent cup. His move ends in accordance with the specific rules of the game he is playing (see below). The opponent then plays likewise from a cup on the opponent's side of the board and the game continues in this way.

Rule 5

The idea of the game is to capture beans, in accordance with the specific rules given below. Captured beans are removed from the main part of the board and placed in the appropriate person's capture storage cup. The winner is the player who captures the most beans.

It is traditional to play all games of Oware at high speed without counting the number of beans in each cup. A single game would normally take 2–4 minutes. A player who is obviously in a losing position may concede the game and resign.

Specific Rules of the Game of Aba-pa

(a) Each player deals the contents of one of his cups round the board, in accordance with General Rule 4. In contrast to other games, the move ends after a single dealing round of the beans.

(b) If the player has selected a cup which contains so many beans (i.e. more than 11) that he arrives back at the original cup in dealing beans round the board, then he must leave the original cup empty. This rule applies if he returns to the original cup a second time (which would happen if his original cup contained more than 22 beans).

(c) If a player's final bean falls into a cup on his opponent's side that contained one or two beans, the player captures the two or three beans that now lie in that cup. The cup into which the last but one bean fell is then examined. If this cup contains two or three beans, then these beans are also captured (provided the cup is on the opponent's side of the board). The next cup (to the player's right) is examined in the same way. Thus the player captures all those beans lying in an unbroken sequence of 2's and 3's on the opponent's side of the board, starting with the cup into which the player's last bean fell and moving to the player's right.

(d) The method of capture described in rule (c) is subject to the restriction that a player is not allowed to capture all the opponent's beans. If he plays a move which would do so, he captures nothing. For example, imagine that the opponent has 1 bean in each of his cups. If the player plays his right-hand cup containing 16 beans, he captures $5 \times 3 = 15$ beans. If the right-hand cup contained 17 beans, then nothing is captured because of rule (d).

(e) If the opponent has no beans on his side and it is the player's turn the player must make a move which will give the opponent one or more beans.

(f) The game ends when either:
    (i) one side of the board is empty and the player on the other side cannot give beans, or
    (ii) if a symmetrical position arises in which both players have a small equal number of beans (up to 3) in corresponding positions in opposite corners of the board. Each player adds

the beans on his side to his captures. (This rule avoids the endless circulation of beans.)

Aba-pa is a 'man's game', and involves considerable strategic skill. It is customary to play a series of 7 games, which would take about 30 minutes when played at traditional speed! This game is widely played in West Africa (Sierra Leone, Togo, Nigeria) with identical rules to those used in Ghana.

Specific Rules of the Game of Apuduo

(a) The player starts dealing beans in accordance with General Rule 4. If the last bean falls into a cup which is not empty, then all the beans in this cup are picked up and dealt round the board in the same way. It is possible (though very unusual) for the player to require more than a hundred individual dealings in order to complete his move. The player's move ends when his last bean falls into an empty cup, on either side of the board.

(b) If the player's last bean falls into an empty cup on his side of the board, then the player captures all the beans in the opposite cup on the opponent's side. In the diagram in which the cups are numbered sequentially, the following pairs of cups are opposite to each other; 1 and 12; 2 and 11; 3 and 10; 4 and 9; 5 and 8; 6 and 7.

(c) In dealing large piles of beans round the board, beans are placed in the cup originally emptied, and beans may in some cases go round the board more than once.

(d) If a move is made which captures all the opponent's beans, the game ends at that point.

(e) If the opponent has no beans on his side of the board and it is the player's turn, the player must make a move which will give the opponent one or more beans if this is possible. If this is not possible, the game ends and the player captures the beans remaining on his side of the board.

This game is most popular with children. Since in many cases it is impossible for a human to calculate the result of a move, the game involves a considerable element of chance. A computer version of Apuduo is available on the Edinburgh Multi-Access System (EMAS).

Specific Rules for the Game of Ananum

(a)   The player starts dealing beans in accordance to General Rule 4.

(b)   If during the deal the number of beans in a cup becomes exactly 4, then these 4 beans are captured by the player on whose side of the board the beans were located.

(c)   If the last bean of a deal makes a 4, the set of 4 beans are captured by the player, irrespective of which side of the board.

(d)   If the last bean of a deal does not
   (i)   make a four
   (ii) fall into an empty cup,
      then the player picks up all the beans in the cup the last bean has landed in, and deals these round the board. One move can therefore consist of a series of deals.

(e)   The player who captures the last but one set of 4 beans (i.e. when there are 8 beans on the board) captures all 8 beans.

Ananum is traditionally a 'woman's game'.

Bao

a Kenyan game

For two players. Make two lines of six or more shallow holes, with a scoring hole at each end.

The game begins with four pebbles in each hole. The first player picks up all the pebbles from any one hole on their side and goes round putting one pebble in each consecutive hole. They then pick up all the pebbles from the hole into which the last pebble was placed, and continue round like this until the last pebble is put into an empty hole.

If that empty hole was on the player's side and there are pebbles in the hole directly opposite, these are collected and placed in that player's 'score hole'. If there are none, or the empty hole was on the other player's side, they score nil.

It is then the other player's turn.

The game continues until there are no pebbles left. The winner is the one with the most pebbles in their score hole.

The direction of movement may be changed between turns.

Editor's note: this is an East African variant of the game of Oware.

Maori draughts

This game is played on the star-shaped design scratched in the sand. Two players each have four stones, marked so they can recognise their own stones. The first player places their stones on points one, two, three and four, whilst the second player places their stones on points five, six, seven and eight.

1 Players make their moves alternately.
2 Only one stone is allowed on each point, or in the centre, at the same time.
3 Players cannot jump one another's stone but can only shift a stone to the centre or to the star point next to it.
4 For the first two moves by each player, only the stones on points one, four, five and eight may be moved.
5 The game is won when one player is blocked by the other so that he cannot move.

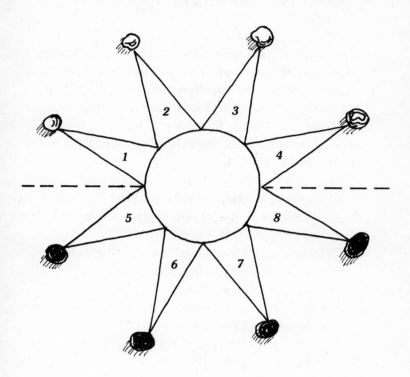

Beds (or Hopscotch)

A design of squares is marked out with a sharp edge of a nail or stone and a peever found, which is a flat piece of stone with a good edge to it. The edge allows one to kick it while standing on one foot.

'A' kicks it into square 1, hops over that square, and proceeds to square 8, then returns down the squares; then kicks it into square 2 and progresses similiarly. If 'A' fails to land the peever in appropriate 'bed' or square, or, while hopping, lands on a line, it becomes B's turn.

Whoever completes, eventually, the 8 'beds' or squares without fault is the winner.

Editor's note: this game, in only slightly different forms, has been noted all over the UK and in Ireland.

Golf

For hundreds of years golf has been the most popular game with the young people in Dornoch, a little cathedral town situated in the Scottish Highlands, fifty miles north of Loch Ness, the loch with the monster.

Golf was played in Dornoch as early as the 16th century. Some think the game began when shepherds tried with their crooks to hit stones into rabbit holes. Walking regularly over the links grass, where their sheep were grazing, it would be the natural thing to try to do. It must have helped pass the time.

Today in Dornoch for £2 a year, local boys and girls can play as many rounds of golf as they want. Not surprisingly many play a great deal. When the British Open Champion, Tom Watson, came to play the famous Royal Dornoch Golf Course, he did something the local children won't forget. He invited several of them to join him in a round of putting. He was surprised, but delighted, to see how good at the game many of them were. They in turn were thrilled to play with their golfing hero.

Index of Games